English
made easy

Key Stage 2
Ages 9–10

Author John Hesk
Consultant Claire White

Certificate

Congratulations to
(write your name here)
for successfully finishing this book.

 You're a star!

DK

Writing dialogue

Use the words below to complete the sentences that follow.

speech marks   paragraph   commas   inverted commas

When each character starts to speak, a new .... begins.

The actual words spoken are enclosed in ...., which are also called

....

Verbs such as said and remarked are separated from the speaker's words by

.... unless there are other punctuation marks in the speech.

Rewrite the following dialogue from **The Wind in the Willows**, inserting the missing speech marks and punctuation.

All complete said the Toad triumphantly, pulling open a larder You see – biscuits potted lobster sardines – everything you can possibly want Soda-water here – baccy there – letter-paper bacon jam cards and dominoes – you'll find he continued, as they descended the steps again you'll find that nothing whatever has been forgotten, when we make our start this afternoon
I beg your pardon said the Rat slowly, as he chewed a straw but did I overhear you say something about 'we' and 'start' and 'this afternoon'
Now, you dear good old Ratty said Toad imploringly don't begin talking in that stiff and sniffy sort of way, because you know you've got to come

....

....

....

....

....

....

....

....

Homophones and homographs

Some words sound the same as other words. Choose words that sound the same to fill in the gaps in each sentence below. ☐D☐
Remember: A **homophone** is a word that sounds the same as another word but has a different meaning and is sometimes spelt differently.
For example: I don't know **where** you are going to **wear** that hat!

Ben asked if he could come t__ the match t__ __,
but we only have t__ __ tickets.

They're fetching t__ __ __ __ jackets from the cloakroom over t__ __ __ __.

W__ __' __ the owner of this coat – I can't tell w__ __ __ __ is w__ __ __ __?

We can't tell w__ __ __ __ __ __ the __ __ __ __ __ __ __ will be dry or wet.

Underline the **homographs** in the sentence below.
Remember: A **homograph** is a word that has the same spelling as another word but has a different meaning.

I went to a football match one cold Saturday. I wore a striped scarf and hat to match. Afterwards, I watched while Mum put a match to the fire.

In the following sentences, the **homographs** are underlined. Read each sentence, and then write another sentence that changes the meaning of the **homograph**.

The old castle had a huge, square <u>keep</u>.

....

I am planning an expedition to the South <u>Pole</u>.

....

Our dog likes me to throw a <u>stick</u>.

....

She won a new computer in the prize <u>draw</u>.

....

He <u>ground</u> the maize to make flour.

....

Puns

Complete this list of **homophones** by writing another word that sounds the same but has a different spelling. ☐D

aloud   *allowed* ....

board   ....

buoy   ....

canon   ....

cereal   ....

chord   ....

course   ....

draught   ....

hair   ....

hoarse   ....

leak   ....

lessen   ....

moor   ....

pale   ....

pause   ....

plane   ....

right   ....

sew   ....

stair   ....

tale   ....

waist   ....

new   ....

pair   ....

bear   ....

Now choose some of the paired words to write **punning** sentences.
Remember: Puns are jokes that rely on **homophones** for their humour.
For example: My pony is a little hoarse today.

....

....

....

....

....

....

Shortened words

Do you know the full forms of these **shortened names**?
Becky   Sue   Katie   Joe   Ben   Nick

Write the full names here in **alphabetical order**.

....

....

Here are some **shortened words**. Write their full version next to the short one.
Use a **dictionary** if you need help. D

bike ....

bus ....

fridge ....

photo ....

hippo ....

o'clock ....

phone ....

Halloween ....

plane ....

pram ....

rhino ....

soccer ....

Acronyms are words made from the first letters of words in longer phrases. Put the first letters of the words in these phrases together to make **acronyms**.

RAdio **D**etection **A**nd **R**anging is shortened to   Radar............................

World **H**ealth **O**rganisation is shortened to ....

Self **C**ontained **U**nderwater **B**reathing **A**pparatus is shortened to ....

Personal **I**dentification **N**umber is shortened to ....

Light **A**mplification by **S**timulated **E**mission of **R**adiation is shortened to ....

Word origins

Many English words originally came from other languages. This means that these words often do not follow English spelling patterns. Look at the words below, and use a **dictionary** to find out which languages they originally came from. Then use your **dictionary** or another **reference book** to find where the languages are spoken. D

	Word	Language	Countries
1	anorak	....	....
2	koala	....	....
3	café	....	....
4	garage	....	....
5	kayak	....	....
6	lieutenant	....	....
7	mayonnaise	....	....
8	sushi	....	....
9	judo	....	....
10	beret	....	....
11	hamburger	....	....
12	spaghetti	....	....
13	khaki	....	....
14	karate	....	....
15	bungalow	....	....
16	ketchup	....	....
17	yoghurt	....	....
18	teepee	....	....
19	restaurant	....	....
20	algebra	....	....

Similes

Some **similes**, such as "like a house on fire", are called **cliches** because they are so overused that they have very little impact. It is a good idea to use new **similes** in your writing, as they attract interest and help your reader to imagine what you are describing. **Remember**: A **simile** is something compared with something else to create an image in the reader's mind. It usually includes the words **like** or **as**.

Practise writing new **similes** by thinking of original comparisons for these **adjectives**.

as light as ..*a petal*.....................   as dry as ....

as good as ....   as heavy as ....

as dull as ....   as pretty as ....

as clean as ....   as big as ....

as quick as ....   as rich as ....

Complete these sentences by thinking of **similes** for the **verbs**.

He crawled like *a snail*............................

The athlete ran like ....

The small boat sank like ....

It rained like ....

Complete these sentences by thinking of **similes** for the **nouns**.

The heat was like *a blazing bonfire*..................

The thick mud felt as if ....

The black smoke smelt like ....

The music she played sounded like ....

The fresh water tasted like ....

The overgrown garden looked as if ....

Prepositions

Here are some useful **prepositions**:

at   by   for   from   in   of   off   on   through   to   up   with
inside   outside   after   towards   underneath   across   except   between

A **preposition** is missing from each of the following sentences. Choose the one that fits best from the list, and write it in the space. You may find that more than one could fit.
Remember: A **preposition** is placed before a word to connect it to other words in a sentence.

The power button was .... the CD drive.

She aimed .... the target.

The ball went .... the window.

I climbed .... the ladder.

Try to hit the ball .... the bat.

We went .... the house when it started to rain.

The cat was hiding .... the bed.

It is one .... the most exciting films I've ever seen.

It's just one thing .... another!

Let's go .... a swim.

Now write ten sentences of your own, using the remaining **prepositions** in the list.

....

....

....

....

....

....

....

....

....

....

Metaphors

Read this **poem** aloud.

What is the Sun?

the Sun is an orange dinghy
    sailing across a calm sea

it is a gold coin
    dropped down a drain in Heaven

the Sun is a yellow beach ball
    kicked high into the summer sky

it is a red thumb-print
    on a sheet of pale blue paper

the Sun is a milk bottle's gold top
    floating in a puddle

Wes Magee

How many **metaphors** for the Sun can you find in this **poem**? Make a list of them below.
Remember: A **metaphor** is something described as if it were something else. It is like
a simile but does not include the words like or as.

an orange dinghy. ....

....

....

Rewrite one of the five **verses**, and change the **metaphor** to a **simile**. To do this, you
only need to add one word.

....

....

....

Pick a **verse** from the **poem**, and write a short paragraph explaining what is meant by
the description of the Sun.

....

....

Which of the **metaphors** in the **poem** seems most effective to you? Why?

....

....

Reading a text

Read this **text**, then answer the questions in full sentences.

The Voice of Nature

An Aboriginal myth from southern Australia relates how, in the beginning, the voice of the Ancestor spoke each day from a great gum tree, and the tribe gathered around to listen. But as time went by the people grew weary of hearing his words of wisdom. One by one they turned their backs on the voice to pursue their own pleasures, and a vast silence settled over the whole of the land and the sea. There was no wind and the tides were still, no birds sang, and the earth seemed to be dying.

The tribe soon wearied of the pleasures of their own making and began to be afraid and lonely. They returned to the great tree again and again, hoping to hear the words that would ease their misery. And one day the voice of their Ancestor spoke again.

He told them it was the last time his voice would be heard, but that he would give them a sign. The great tree split open, a huge tongue of light came down into its trunk, and then it closed up again.

Since that time the Aboriginals have known that the voice of their Ancestor exists in all things, and speaks to them through every part of nature.

From *Dreamtime Heritage* by A. & M. J. Roberts

Why did the tribe traditionally gather around the great gum tree?

....

....

Why did the people abandon this custom (stop going to the tree)?

....

....

What happened to the natural world when the people broke this tradition?

....

....

What feelings made the people return to the tree?

....

....

Reading and understanding

Reread the **text** on page 10, then answer the following questions in full sentences.

What is an **ancestor**? ☐D

....

....

Describe the sign given to the people by the Ancestor. Explain the meaning of the sign.

....

....

....

The Australian gum tree has a **scientific** name. Use **reference books** or a **computer** to find out what it is, and write it here.

....

Explain the word **tribe**. What do we mean by **tribal society**? ☐D

....

....

What evidence can you find in the text to suggest that **nature** was important to the people? Can you explain why this was?

....

....

Use a **dictionary** to find out what the saying "up a gum tree" means. ☐D

....

....

What does this passage make you feel?
Which words make you feel like this?

....

....

....

A traditional story

Read this **story** from India about a tree, and answer the questions in full sentences. The writer explains that, as a child, she often heard this story told on a special day in August – the Day for Brothers – when "all sisters in India pray that no harm comes to their brothers".

The Mango Tree (Part One)

In a small town, there was a small house in which lived a young man, his wife, and the young man's sister. This small house had a small garden at the back in which grew a small mango tree. One day the young man's wife came to him and said, "Look here, I'm fed up with our situation. Your sister …"

"Have you come here to complain about my sister again?"

"What can I do? I know it's quite useless … My complaints fall on deaf ears, anyway … I'm just … so angry with your sister. I get up early in the morning, draw water from the well, light the fire in the kitchen, cook breakfast, wash and scrub pots …"

"Don't go on," said the brother. "I've heard it all before."

"And what does your lazy sister do all day? Nothing … nothing … she lolls about in the garden, watering her mango tree, talking to it, clearing away dead leaves, and feeding it manure and mulch …"

"That isn't all she does. She comes in and talks to me. Just an hour ago, she was playing chess with me."

"Just because she adores you, doesn't mean you should ignore her faults. You must tell her to leave that … silly mango tree alone, and come and help me with the housework. I really think we should marry her off. That might teach her to be more responsible."

Since the sister was of marriageable age, the brother could not really object. He knew though, that he would miss her very, very much.

A marriage was arranged.

Why did the young man's wife complain to him?

....

....

What does the writer mean when she writes that the marriage was arranged?

....

....

Now read part two of the **story** that began on page 12, then answer the questions.

The Mango Tree (Part Two)

When all the ceremonies were over, and the sister was about to leave with her groom to lead a new life in a new town, she turned to her sister-in-law and said, "Dearest sister-in-law, I'm going to miss my mango tree so much. Would you please do me a great favour and look after it for me? Please water it well and clear the weeds that grow in its shadow."

"Oh, well, yes, yes," answered the sister-in-law.

Once the sister had left, the sister-in-law turned to her husband and yelled, "Did you hear that? Did you *hear* that? Did you hear your selfish sister? She didn't say that she was going to miss you. She didn't say that she was going to miss me. She *did* say that she was going to miss her mango tree!" She decided then that she was going to ignore the mango tree. The mango tree irritated her just as much as her husband's sister had. Now she could be rid of both.

As the days passed, the unwatered, uncared for mango tree started drying up and its leaves began to fall.

At the same time, the brother, who had been a strong, robust and healthy young man, began to lose his appetite and get thinner and weaker.

One day, a letter arrived. It was from the sister and said, "Dearest brother and sister-in-law. I hope all is well and that my tree is green, and that my brother is in good health."

The remaining leaves of the mango tree were quite yellow by this time, but the sister-in-law wrote back, "Dearest sister. Your tree is fine, but your brother has not been feeling so good."

Soon another letter arrived from the sister. "Are you sure my tree is green? And how is my brother?"

Why did the young man's wife object when his sister said that she would miss her mango tree?

....

....

Explain why the young man's wife neglected the tree.

....

....

Which words in the story so far would you use in your own writing, and why?

....

....

A traditional story (continued)

Read part three of the **story**, then answer the questions.

The Mango Tree (Part Three)

The mango tree only had one brown leaf on it now, and the brother was so sick that the doctors had said that he could not live. So the sister-in-law wrote back, "Your tree is fine, but the doctors have given up all hopes for your brother."

When the sister received this letter, she raced back to her small home town and went straight into the small garden to water her small tree. As she watered it, cleared the weeds around it, and mulched it, it began slowly to turn green.

The brother too, began to recover.

As more leaves returned to the tree, the brother's cheeks got pinker and his eyes became brighter. Within a month, the tree was healthy and strong.

And so was the brother.

It was only then that the sister turned to her sister-in-law and said, "Now do you understand? It was not the tree that I loved, but my brother. It was not the tree whose welfare I was concerned with, but my brother's. The tree and my brother share a common soul. It was my duty to look after them both."

From *Seasons of Splendour* by Madhur Jaffrey

Can you explain what "the tree and my brother share a common soul" might mean?

....

....

....

How do you think the sister knew that the wife was lying when she said the tree was fine?

....

....

....

Of the three characters in this **story**, whose opinions and feelings do we learn most about?

....

....

Your own retelling

Reread the **story** on pages 12, 13 and 14, then write a **story**, a **letter**, a **monologue** for a play, or a **poem**. Write this from either the brother's or sister's **point of view**. You might find it easier if you imagine that you are the **character** you have chosen.

....

....

....

....

....

....

....

....

....

....

....

....

....

....

....

Possessives and plurals

A **possessive apostrophe** shows us who or what belongs to somebody or something.

> We usually write **the brothers of Madhur** as **Madhur's brothers**,
> and we write **the sister of the brothers** as the **brothers' sister**.

The **apostrophe** is always placed after the word that is "owning".
Always add an **-s** if the owner is **singular**.
Always add an **-s** if the owners are **plural** and don't end in an s.
Do **not** add an **-s** if the owners are **plural** and already **end** in an s.

> Write the **friend of Thomas** as **Thomas's friend**.
> Write the **ball of the boys** as **boys' ball**.

Rewrite the **phrases** below so that they include a **possessive apostrophe**. The first one has been done for you.

the mango tree of his sister	*his sister's mango tree*
the wives of the men	
the beliefs of the tribe	
the fruit of the trees	
the wisdom of the Ancestor	
the roots of the mango tree	
the saris of the women	
the opinion of my sister	
the branches of the trees	

These **phrases** work in the same way, although you might not think so! Rewrite them.

in the time of three days	*in three days' time*
in the time of one hour	
in the time of two weeks	

Clauses

A **clause** is part of a sentence. A **clause** must contain a **verb** (a doing or being word). The **main clause** in a sentence makes sense on its own; it can usually be written as a sentence by itself. A **subordinate** clause gives further meaning to the **main clause** but does not make complete sense on its own.

Look at this sentence.

As time went by, the people grew weary of hearing the words of wisdom.

The **main clause** is "the people grew weary of hearing the words of wisdom" – it could be a sentence on its own. The **subordinate clause** is "as time went by" – it is not a complete sentence on its own.

Write down the **main** and **subordinate clauses** in the sentences below.

When she received the letter, the sister raced back to the small house in her old home town.

main clause: ....

....

subordinate clause: ....

Hoping to hear the words that would ease their misery, the people returned to the great tree again and again.

main clause: ....

subordinate clause: ....

....

As the days passed, the unwatered, uncared for mango tree started drying up and its leaves began to fall.

main clause: ....

....

subordinate clause: ....

17

Understanding poetry

Read this **poem** aloud.

The Rabbit

We are going to see the rabbit.
We are going to see the rabbit.
Which rabbit, people say?
Which rabbit, ask the children?
Which rabbit?
The only rabbit,
The only rabbit in England,
Sitting behind a barbed-wire fence
Under the floodlights, neon lights,
Sodium lights,
Nibbling grass
On the only patch of grass
In England, in England
(Except the grass by the hoardings
Which doesn't count.)
We are going to see the rabbit
And we must be there on time.

First we shall go by escalator,
Then we shall go by underground,
And then we shall go by motorway
And then by helicopterway,
And the last ten yards we shall have to go
On foot.

And now we are going
All the way to see the rabbit,
We are nearly there,
We are longing to see it,
And so is the crowd
Which is here in thousands
With mounted policemen
And big loudspeakers
And bands and banners,
And everyone has come a long way.
But soon we shall see it
Sitting and nibbling
The blades of grass
On the only patch of grass
In – but something has gone wrong!
Why is everyone so angry,
Why is everyone jostling
And slanging and complaining?

The rabbit has gone,
Yes, the rabbit has gone.
He has actually burrowed down into
    the earth
And made himself a warren, under
    the earth,
Despite all these people.
And what shall we do?
What *can* we do?

It is all a pity, you must be disappointed,
Go home and do something else for today,
Go home again, go home for today.
For you cannot hear the rabbit, under the earth,
Remarking rather sadly to himself, by himself,
As he rests in his warren, under the earth:
'It won't be long, they are bound to come,
They are bound to come and find me, even here.'

Alan Brownjohn

Reading and understanding

Reread the **poem** on page 18, then answer the following questions in full sentences.

Is this **poem** about the past, the present or the future? What evidence is there in the poem for your answer?

....

....

Why do you think that this is the only rabbit on the only patch of grass?

....

....

What is a hoarding? D

....

....

Five ways of travelling are mentioned in the **poem**. What are they? Which is least harmful to the environment?

....

....

Find the **noun** that names the rabbit's home, then write another word for a rabbit's home. D
Remember: A **noun** is a naming word.

....

Can you name the wild animals that live in a **sett**, an **earth** and a **holt**. D

....

....

Why is the rabbit sad?

....

....

In some places rabbits are regarded as pests. What does this mean?

....

....

Persuasive arguments

Read this example of **informative** and **persuasive** writing.

1 Homes for others

Every living creature has a place where it feels at home. Polar bears are at home in the Arctic; lions are at home in the African grasslands. The place where a creature feels at home is called its natural habitat. You feel at home in your own house. You have safe food to eat and you may know your neighbours, even if you are not friends with all of them. It is the same for all other creatures. Their natural habitat is a place where they and their ancestors have lived for perhaps millions of years. They are used to the climate and the other species in the same habitat. Very often wild creatures can only live in one sort of habitat. Conservationists began by saving species which were threatened by stopping hunting, poaching, or overfishing. Now, people realise that saving a species is not enough. Its home has to be saved as well. Natural habitats are in danger everywhere. When people cut down forests or drain swamps the creatures which lived in those habitats may have nowhere else to go.

2 Why conserve?

We are faced with an important decision. We know that thousands of different species are threatened with becoming extinct. Once they are gone, they will never come back. There are probably thousands more in existence that we don't know about because we haven't discovered them yet. Conservation can save some of these species, but costs money and affects people's lives. Why should we bother with it?

3 Looking after ourselves

We need the other creatures in the biosphere because they provide us with food, clothing, building materials, fuel and medicine. However we must use these carefully and sparingly. If we destroy the biosphere because we are greedy or just stupid, then we will die out ourselves. If we look after it, we shall survive, and so will all the other creatures. So conserving the biosphere means looking after ourselves.

From *Endangered Earth* by Jeremy Burgess

What effect do you think the **headings** of the **paragraphs** have on the reader?

....

....

....

Writing a summary

Write out as a list the first sentence in each **paragraph** on page 20.

1 Every living creature ....

....

2 ....

3 ....

....

Read these sentences again, then **summarise** (write a shortened version of) the writer's argument. Try to write it in 150 words or less, without leaving out any of the main ideas.

....

....

....

....

....

....

....

....

....

....

....

....

....

....

....

....

....

....

More persuasive writing

Reread the **text** on page 20, then answer the following questions in full sentences.

How does the author explain the term **natural habitat**?

....

....

The author tells you how you feel in your house – but does he really know? Why do you think he does this?

....

....

The author says that *natural habitats are in danger everywhere*. Is this true or not? Why does he say this?

....

....

How many times does the author use the words **we**, **us** or **ourselves** in paragraphs 2 and 3? Why do you think he does this?

....

....

The author says that if we look after the biosphere, we will survive and so will all the other creatures. Do you think this is definitely true, or can you think of other possible threats to people and animals?

....

....

Write down other **words** or **phrases** (groups of words) that could replace these words in the article without changing its meaning. ☐D ☐T

poaching ....

extinct ....

biosphere ....

habitat ....

conservation ....

Conservation dictionary

Make your own **conservation dictionary** by collecting words to do with **conservation** and the prevention of **pollution**. Here are some words to start you off.

pollution   conservation   smog   litter   species

waste   atmosphere   fossil fuels   environment

Now find some more words yourself, and write them here. You may want to use **reference books**, the **Internet** or **CD-ROMs** to help you. T

....

....

....

Put the **conservation** words in **alphabetical order**, and write a short **meaning** for each one. The **meaning** should be easy to understand. The first one has been done for you. D

Word	Meaning
atmosphere	The layer of gases that surrounds the Earth.

Letter of complaint

Read this **letter**, then answer in full sentences the questions that follow.

Parkview,
Green Lane,
Greenford
11th April

The Chairman,
Greenford Council

Dear Sir,

I am writing to complain about the state of the waste ground, formerly known as Greenford Park, which can be seen from the front of my house.

I use the word "waste" deliberately as this, in truth, is what it has become.

Are we, as local residents, expected to suffer the misuse and probable ruination of this once useful, attractive amenity without expressing our feelings?

For the last month, I have noted the following thoughtless actions that have contributed to its present condition:

- the casual dropping of litter in the form of cans, fast-food packaging, etc.,
- the deliberate dumping of an old mattress,
- damage to the few remaining trees and wild plants from vehicles either crossing the area or parking on it,
- the careless behaviour of dog owners who allow their pets to foul the area without any attempt to clear up the mess that remains, thus endangering public health.

Added to these obvious forms of pollution, there is the noise from portable "music-making" devices in fine weather, which must contribute to the disappearance of the rabbits, badgers and other species from this once beautifully unspoilt wild area.

In these days of conservation and "green" awareness, I should have thought that our council might leap at the chance to create an area that would promote the preservation of plants and wildlife.

Yours faithfully,
Mr I. M. Wild

What is the writer's reason for writing? In which paragraph does he first state his reason?

....

....

Why does Mr Wild use inverted commas around the word "music-making"?

....

....

Reading and understanding

Answer the following questions about the **letter** on page 24.

How does the writer suggest that he is writing on behalf of everyone living in Greenford?

....

....

How does the writer make clear his four main complaints? What are they?

....

....

....

Why does Mr Wild use words such as **casual, deliberate, thoughtless** and **careless**?

....

....

The writer is trying to persuade the council to do something. Which words or phrases suggest this?

....

....

Is this just a **letter of complaint**, or does it make any suggestions for improvement? If so, what are they?

....

....

A **rhetorical question** is used to make people think, and an answer is not usually expected. Can you find the **rhetorical question** in this **letter** and write it here?

....

....

Do you think this letter will be successful? Why do you think this?

....

....

....

....

Read this **poster**. Decide whether or not it will persuade people to take an interest.

PUBLIC MEETING

In the Village Hall at 7.00 PM
on Wednesday 15th April

OUR PARK IS OUR PROBLEM!

Do you care about:
Our plants and animals?
Natural beauty?
Conservation?

If you really do care then...
Come along to this meeting
Express your views
Sign our petition
Write to your councillor and MP

Something must be done before it's too late!

Now write a short **paragraph** saying what you think is **effective** or **ineffective** about
this **poster**.

....
....
....
....
....
....
....
....

Newspaper report

Imagine you are a reporter working for the local paper. You have been asked to write a brief **report** about what happened at the meeting advertised on the poster on page 26. You have limited space for your report, and the editor has already decided on the headline (see below).

You must include:
- when and where the meeting took place
- the name of the chairperson and the number of people attending
- a summary of the views and feelings expressed
- any possible outcomes (what might happen next)

A Public Problem

....

....

....

....

....

....

....

....

....

....

....

....

....

....

....

....

....

Reading a classic novel

In the nineteenth century, some writers wanted their readers to understand more about the lives of others. In those days before television and the Internet, books were one of the most important ways of **persuading** people to think about the rest of the world.

In Chapters 5 and 17 of his novel *Hard Times*, Charles Dickens describes Coketown, an industrial city in the north of England. Read his description of Coketown in these **extracts**.

It was a town of red brick, or of brick that would have been red if the smoke and ashes had allowed it; … It was a town of machinery and tall chimneys, out of which interminable serpents of smoke trailed themselves for ever and ever, and never got uncoiled. It had a black canal in it, and a river that ran purple with ill-smelling dye, and vast piles of building full of windows where there was a rattling and a trembling all day long, and where the piston of the steam-engine worked monotonously up and down, like the head of an elephant in a state of melancholy madness. It contained several large streets all very like one another, and many small streets still more like one another, inhabited by people equally like one another, who all went in and out at the same hours, with the same sound upon the same pavements, to do the same work, and to whom every day was the same as yesterday and tomorrow, and every year the counterpart of the last and the next.

… The streets were hot and dusty on the summer day, and the sun was so bright that it even shone through the heavy vapour drooping over Coketown, and could not be looked at steadily. Stokers emerged from low underground doorways into factory yards, and sat on steps, and posts, and palings, wiping their swarthy visages, and contemplating coals. The whole town seemed to be frying in oil. There was a stifling smell of hot oil everywhere. The steam-engines shone with it, the dresses of the Hands were soiled with it, the mills throughout their many storeys oozed and trickled it … their inhabitants, wasting with heat, toiled languidly in the desert. But no temperature made the melancholy-mad elephants more mad or more sane. Their wearisome heads went up and down at the same rate in hot weather and cold, wet weather and dry, fair weather and foul. The measured motion of their shadows on the walls, was the substitute Coketown had to show for the shadows of rustling woods; while, for the summer hum of insects, it could offer, all the year round, from the dawn of Monday to the night of Saturday, the whirr of shafts and wheels.

Reading and understanding

Answer these questions about the **extracts** on page 28.

Charles Dickens uses more detail than many modern writers would. Why do you think this is?

....

....

Dickens uses many long sentences and repeats words. What effect does this have on the reader?

....

....

Find as many **adjectives** describing **colours**, **sounds** and **smells** as you can.
Write them here.
Remember: An **adjective** is a describing word.

....

....

....

Find a **metaphor** for smoke and write it here.
Remember: A writer uses a **metaphor** to describe something as if it were something else.

....

Find a **simile** for a steam-engine and write it here.
Remember: A **simile** is used to compare one thing with another to create an image in the reader's mind. It often includes the words **like** or **as**.

....

Here are some of the words that you may have found unfamiliar or difficult. Draw a line to match each one with its meaning. The first one has been done for you. ☐D

interminable	very sad
monotonously	leaked slowly
melancholy	endless
counterpart	weakly
wearisome	same
stokers	in the same dull way
visage	furnace feeders
oozed	boring and tiring
languidly	face

Reading another classic novel

Charles Dickens also wrote *David Copperfield*, a novel about a man's life. As a young boy, David is treated harshly by his stepfather and bullied at school. At the age of ten, he is sent to London to work. Being clever and ambitious, he finds the work very boring. Here, the grown-up David Copperfield describes that particular period in his life.

... I became, at ten years old, a little labouring hind in the service of Murdstone and Grinby.

Murdstone and Grinby's warehouse was at the water side. It was down in Blackfriars ... it was the last house at the bottom of a narrow street, curving down hill to the river, with some stairs at the end, where people took boats. It was a crazy old house with a wharf of its own, abutting on the water when the tide was in, and on the mud when the tide was out, and literally over-run with rats. Its panelled rooms, discoloured with the dirt and smoke of a hundred years, I dare say; its decaying floors and staircase, the squeaking and scuffling of the old grey rats down in the cellars; and the dirt and rottenness of the place; are things, not of many years ago, in my mind, but of the present instant. They are all before me, just as they were in the evil hour when I went among them for the first time. ...

Murdstone and Grinby's trade was among a good many kinds of people, but an important branch of it was the supply of wines and spirits to certain packet ships. ... I think there were some among them that made voyages both to the East and West Indies. I know that a great many empty bottles were one of the consequences of this traffic, and that certain men and boys were employed to examine them against the light, and reject those that were flawed, and to rinse and wash them. When the empty bottles ran short, there were labels to be pasted on full ones, or corks to be fitted to them, or seals to be put upon the corks, or finished bottles to be packed in casks. All this work was my work, and of the boys employed upon it I was one.

Name the **narrator** of this part of the story. D

....

Explain the difference between a **narrator** and an **author**. D

....

....

....

Reading and understanding

Answer these questions about the **extract** on page 30.

The third **paragraph** describes the kind of work that the men and boys did.
Can you explain briefly what it was?

....

....

Can you complete these **old words** and **phrases** from the extract? They match the
meanings of the **modern words** given below. D

Modern word	Old word
next to	ab __ __ __ __ __ g
rotting	d __ __ __ __ __ __ g
now	of the p __ __ __ __ __ __ i __ __ __ __ __ __ t
journeys	vo __ __ __ __ s
a lot of	a gr __ __ t m __ __ y
results	co __ __ __ __ __ __ __ __ __ s
damaged	f __ __ __ __ d
put on	put __ __ __ __ __

A **hind** was a servant who lived in a house belonging to the master or mistress. Why is
this word used in the first sentence?

....

....

Do you think this **description** gives the reader a good idea of the way David felt? What
words can you think of to describe his feelings about his life and work at this time?

....

....

Connectives

Here are some one-word **connectives**.

and	but	when	because
so	for	as	though

Choose a different one of these **connectives** to link each of the paired sentences below.
Remember: **Connectives** are words or phrases that link together different parts of a text.
Connectives that link sentences, clauses or parts of phrases are called **conjunctions**.

I fell over. I hurt my knee. ....

....

The game ended. The referee blew his whistle. ....

....

She couldn't ride her bike. It had a puncture. ....

....

I couldn't spell that word. I fetched the dictionary. ....

....

We arrived on time. The train was delayed. ....

....

Here are some **words** and **phrases** that can also be used as **connectives**.

also	however	this means	for example	as this

Fit the **connectives** above into the spaces in these three paragraphs.

    Many kinds of words can be used to connect ideas in a piece of writing.
F__r e__ __ __ __ __ __, pronouns, adverbs, and conjunctions are all useful.

    T__ __ __ __ __ __s that we can make our writing more varied and
more interesting to read. A__ __o, the words we choose can help us to make
our meaning clearer to our readers.

    H__ __ __ __ __r, we should try not to use too many of these connectives
in a short piece, __s __ __ __s can make our sentences long and confusing.

Answer Section with Parents' Notes

Key Stage 2
Ages 9–10

This 8-page section provides answers or explanatory notes to all the activities in this book. This will enable you to assess your child's work.

Point out any spelling mistakes, incorrect punctuation and grammatical errors as you mark each page. Also correct any handwriting errors. (Your child should use the handwriting style taught at his or her school.) As well as making corrections, it is very important to praise your child's efforts and achievements.

Encourage your child to use a dictionary, and suggest that he or she uses a notebook to compile a **word bank** of new words or difficult spellings.

2

Writing dialogue

Use the words below to complete the sentences that follow.

speech marks   paragraph   commas   inverted commas

When each character starts to speak, a new .... paragraph .... begins.

The actual words spoken are enclosed in ..... speech marks ....., which are also called ... inverted commas ... .

Verbs such as said and remarked are separated from the speaker's words by .... commas .... unless there are other punctuation marks in the speech.

Rewrite the following dialogue from **The Wind in the Willows**, inserting the missing speech marks and punctuation.

All complete said the Toad triumphantly, pulling open a larder You see – biscuits potted lobster sardines – everything you can possibly want Soda-water here – baccy there – letter-paper bacon jam cards and dominoes – you'll find he continued, as they descended the steps again you'll find that nothing whatever has been forgotten, when we make our start this afternoon

I beg your pardon said the Rat slowly, as he chewed a straw but did I overhear you say something about 'we' and 'start' and 'this afternoon'

Now, you dear good old Ratty said Toad imploringly don't begin talking in that stiff and sniffy sort of way, because you know you've got to come

.... "All complete," said the Toad triumphantly, pulling open a larder. "You see – biscuits, potted lobster, sardines – everything you can possibly want. Soda-water here – baccy there – letter-paper, bacon, jam, cards and dominoes – you'll find," he continued, as they descended the steps again, "you'll find that nothing whatever has been forgotten, when we make our start this afternoon."

.... "I beg your pardon," said the Rat slowly, as he chewed a straw, "but did I overhear you say something about 'we' and 'start' and 'this afternoon'?"

.... "Now, you dear good old Ratty," said Toad imploringly, "don't begin talking in that stiff and sniffy sort of way, because you know you've got to come."

This activity helps your child to recognise direct speech and the correct punctuation used to set it out. Check that your child has completed the sentences correctly, before applying this knowledge to the piece of dialogue from *The Wind in the Willows*.

3

Homophones and homographs

Some words sound the same as other words. Choose words that sound the same to fill in the gaps in each sentence below. D
Remember: A homophone is a word that sounds the same as another word but has a different meaning and is sometimes spelt differently.
For example: I don't know **where** you are going to **wear** that hat!

Ben asked if he could come t o the match t o o , but we only have t w o tickets.

They're fetching t h e i r jackets from the cloakroom over t h e r e .

W h o ' s the owner of this coat – I can't tell w h o s e is w h o s e ?

We can't tell w h e t h e r the w e a t h e r will be dry or wet.

Underline the **homographs** in the sentence below.
Remember: A homograph is a word that has the same spelling as another word but has a different meaning.

I went to a football match one cold Saturday. I wore a striped scarf and hat to match. Afterwards, I watched while Mum put a match to the fire.

In the following sentences, the **homographs** are underlined. Read each sentence, and then write another sentence that changes the meaning of the **homograph**.

The old castle had a huge, square keep.

....

I am planning an expedition to the South Pole.

....

Our dog likes me to throw a stick.

....

She won a new computer in the prize draw.

....

He ground the maize to make flour.

....

Answers may vary

On this page your child practises using some common homophones and homographs. Children often find these words confusing, so you may need to offer help with these exercises. Remember to praise your child's correct answers.

4

Puns

Complete this list of **homophones** by writing another word that sounds the same but has a different spelling. D

aloud	allowed	board	bored
buoy	boy	canon	cannon
cereal	serial	chord	cord
course	coarse	draught	draft
hair	hare	hoarse	horse
leak	leek	lessen	lesson
moor	more	pale	pail
pause	paws	plane	plain
right	write	sew	so
stair	stare	tale	tail
waist	waste	new	knew
pair	pear	bear	bare

Now choose some of the paired words to write **punning** sentences.
Remember: Puns are jokes that rely on **homophones** for their humour.
For example: My pony is a little hoarse today.

....

....

....

....

....

Answers may vary

The exercises on this page provide further practice with homophones. Check that your child writes his or her puns in complete sentences and selects the correct homophone for each context. Encourage him or her to have fun with this activity.

Shortened words

Do you know the full forms of these **shortened names**?
Becky Sue Katie Joe Ben Nick

Write the full names here in **alphabetical order**.

Benjamin, Joseph, Katherine, Nicholas, Rebecca, Susan

Here are some **shortened words**. Write their full version next to the short one.
Use a **dictionary** if you need help. D

bike	bicycle
bus	omnibus

fridge	refrigerator
photo	photograph

hippo	hippopotamus
o'clock	of the clock

phone	telephone
Halloween	All Hallows' Eve

plane	aeroplane
pram	perambulator

rhino	rhinoceros
soccer	Association football

Acronyms are words made from the first letters of words in longer phrases. Put the first letters of the words in these phrases together to make **acronyms**.

RAdio Detection And Ranging is shortened to Radar

World Health Organisation is shortened to WHO

Self Contained Underwater Breathing Apparatus is shortened to Scuba

Personal Identification Number is shortened to PIN

Light Amplification by Stimulated Emission of Radiation is shortened to Laser

The fun activities on this page allow your child to find out how short words are created from longer words and phrases. Talk about the "living" nature of languages – how languages change and develop.

Word origins

Many English words originally came from other languages. This means that these words often do not follow English spelling patterns. Look at the words below, and use a **dictionary** to find out which languages they originally came from. Then use your **dictionary** or another **reference book** to find where the languages are spoken. D

	Word	Language	Countries
1	anorak	Inuit	Greenland
2	koala	Aboriginal	Australia
3	café	French	France
4	garage	French	France
5	kayak	Inuit	Greenland
6	lieutenant	French	France
7	mayonnaise	French	France
8	sushi	Japanese	Japan
9	judo	Japanese	Japan
10	beret	French	France
11	hamburger	German	Germany
12	spaghetti	Italian	Italy
13	khaki	Urdu	Persia (Iran)
14	karate	Japanese	Japan
15	bungalow	Hindi	India, Bangladesh
16	ketchup	Chinese	China
17	yoghurt	Turkish	Turkey
18	teepee	Siouan	N. America
19	restaurant	French	France
20	algebra	Arabic	Saudi Arabia, Kuwait

Pages 6 and 7 encourage your child to look at English words that originate from other languages. Some dictionaries may disagree with these answers – explain that it can be difficult to determine a word's exact origin, but that this makes the "detective work" fun.

Similes

Some **similes**, such as "like a house on fire", are called **cliches** because they are so overused that they have very little impact. It is a good idea to use new **similes** in your writing, as they attract interest and help your reader to imagine what you are describing.
Remember: A **simile** is something compared with something else to create an image in the reader's mind. It usually includes the words **like** or **as**.

Practise writing new **similes** by thinking of original comparisons for these **adjectives**.

as light as a petal	as dry as
as good as	as heavy as
as dull as	as pretty as
as clean as	as big as
as quick as	as rich as

Answers may vary

Complete these sentences by thinking of **similes** for the **verbs**.

He crawled like a snail

The athlete ran like

The small boat sank like

It rained like

Answers may vary

Complete these sentences by thinking of **similes** for the **nouns**.

The heat was like a blazing bonfire

The thick mud felt as if

The black smoke smelt like

The music she played sounded like

The fresh water tasted like

The overgrown garden looked as if

Answers may vary

These activities encourage your child to think of original comparisons and to avoid overused expressions. There are no right or wrong answers to these questions – accept any original similes as long as they include the words *like* or *as*.

Prepositions

Here are some useful **prepositions**:
at by for from in off on through to up with
inside outside after towards underneath across except between

A **preposition** is missing from each of the following sentences. Choose the one that fits best from the list, and write it in the space. You may find that more than one could fit.
Remember: A **preposition** is placed before a word to connect it to other words in a sentence.

The power button was underneath the CD drive.

She aimed at the target.

The ball went through the window.

I climbed up the ladder.

Try to hit the ball with the bat.

We went inside the house when it started to rain.

The cat was hiding underneath the bed.

It is one of the most exciting films I've ever seen.

It's just one thing after another!

Let's go for a swim.

Now write ten sentences of your own, using the remaining **prepositions** in the list.

Answers may vary

These exercises will help your child to appreciate the wide range of prepositions and to understand their function in sentences. Talk about your child's sentences to consolidate his or her understanding and knowledge.

Metaphors

Read this **poem** aloud.

What is the Sun?

the Sun is an orange dinghy
sailing across a calm sea

it is a gold coin
dropped down a drain in Heaven

the Sun is a yellow beach ball
kicked high into the summer sky

it is a red thumb-print
on a sheet of pale blue paper

the Sun is a milk bottle's gold top
floating in a puddle

Wes Magee

How many **metaphors** for the Sun can you find in this **poem**? Make a list of them below.
Remember: A metaphor is something described as if it were something else. It is like a simile but does not include the words like or as.

an orange dinghy, a gold chain, a yellow beach ball, a red thumb-print,
a milk bottle's gold top

Rewrite one of the five **verses**, and change the **metaphor** to a **simile**. To do this, you only need to add one word.

e.g. the Sun is like an orange dinghy

sailing across a calm sea Answers may vary

Pick a **verse** from the **poem**, and write a short paragraph explaining what is meant by the description of the Sun.

Answers may vary

Which of the **metaphors** in the **poem** seems most effective to you? Why?

Answers may vary

This page helps your child to appreciate how metaphor works and to differentiate between metaphor and simile. Again, the questions are open-ended – accept any answers that can be sensibly argued from the poem.

Reading a text

Read this **text**, then answer the questions in full sentences.

The Voice of Nature

An Aboriginal myth from southern Australia relates how, in the beginning, the voice of the Ancestor spoke each day from a great gum tree, and the tribe gathered around to listen. But as time went by the people grew weary of hearing his words of wisdom. One by one they turned their backs on the voice to pursue their own pleasures, and a vast silence settled over the whole of the land and the sea. There was no wind and the tides were still, no birds sang, and the earth seemed to be dying.

The tribe soon wearied of the pleasures of their own making and began to be afraid and lonely. They returned to the great tree again and again, hoping to hear the words that would ease their misery. And one day the voice of their Ancestor spoke again.

He told them it was the last time his voice would be heard, but that he would give them a sign. The great tree split open, a huge tongue of light came down into its trunk, and then it closed up again.

Since that time the Aboriginals have known that the voice of their Ancestor exists in all things, and speaks to them through every part of nature.

From *Dreamtime Heritage* by A. & M. J. Roberts

Why did the tribe traditionally gather around the great gum tree?
The tribe used to gather around the tree to hear the Ancestor speak.

Why did the people abandon this custom (stop going to the tree)?
They abandoned the custom because they grew weary of hearing the Ancestor's
words of wisdom.

What happened to the natural world when the people broke this tradition?
When people broke this tradition, there was no wind or tides, no birds sang,
and the earth seemed to be dying.

What feelings made the people return to the tree?
Feelings of fear and loneliness made them return to the tree.

The National Curriculum for English requires your child to examine a range of texts from different cultures. Listen to your child read the extract, and help him or her with difficult words. Then discuss the customs and beliefs of this tribe.

Reading and understanding

Reread the **text** on page 10, then answer the following questions in full sentences.

What is an **ancestor**? D
An ancestor is someone from whom a person is descended.

Describe the sign given to the people by the Ancestor. Explain the meaning of the sign.
The great tree split open, a huge tongue of light came down into its trunk, and
then it closed up again. This was a sign that the Ancestor is present in all
things and speaks to the people through every part of nature.

The Australian gum tree has a **scientific** name. Use **reference books** or a **computer** to find out what it is, and write it here.
Eucalyptus

Explain the word **tribe**. What do we mean by **tribal society**? D
A tribe is a group of people with common ancestors. Tribal society is a society
organised around the culture and rules of a tribe.

What evidence can you find in the text to suggest that **nature** was important to the people? Can you explain why this was?
The people felt afraid and lonely when the earth seemed to be dying.
They gathered round the gum tree every day to listen to their Ancestor.

Use a **dictionary** to find out what the saying "up a gum tree" means. D
The saying "up a gum tree" means to be in a very
awkward or difficult position.

What does this passage make you feel?
Which words make you feel like this?

Answers may vary

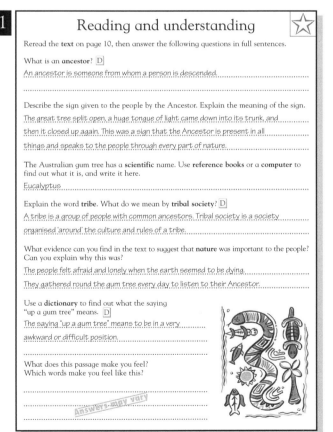

The questions on this page refer to the extract on page 10. Encourage your child to develop good research skills. He or she could use reference books, CD-ROMs or the Internet, which should all be available at your local library.

A traditional story

Read this **story** from India about a tree, and answer the questions in full sentences. The writer explains that, as a child, she often heard this story told on a special day in August – the Day for Brothers – when "all sisters in India pray that no harm comes to their brothers".

The Mango Tree (Part One)

In a small town, there was a small house in which lived a young man, his wife, and the young man's sister. This small house had a small garden at the back in which grew a small mango tree. One day the young man's wife came to him and said, "Look here, I'm fed up with our situation. Your sister …"

"Have you come here to complain about my sister again?"

"What can I do? I know it's quite useless … My complaints fall on deaf ears, anyway … I'm just … so angry with your sister. I get up early in the morning, draw water from the well, light the fire in the kitchen, cook breakfast, wash and scrub pots …"

"Don't go on," said the brother. "I've heard it all before."

"And what does your lazy sister do all day? Nothing … nothing … she lolls about in the garden, watering her mango tree, talking to it, clearing away dead leaves, and feeding it manure and mulch …"

"That isn't all she does. She comes in and talks to me. Just an hour ago, she was playing chess with me."

"Just because she adores you, doesn't mean you should ignore her faults. You must tell her to leave that … silly mango tree alone, and come and help me with the housework. I really think we should marry her off. That might teach her to be more responsible."

Since the sister was of marriageable age, the brother could not really object. He knew though, that he would miss her very, very much.

A marriage was arranged.

Why did the young man's wife complain to him?
She complained because the young man's sister did nothing all
day except care for the mango tree.

What does the writer mean when she writes that the marriage was arranged?
The sister's marriage was arranged by her brother and
sister-in-law. They chose the groom and organised the wedding.

Pages 12 to 15 provide your child with a further opportunity to investigate text from another culture. The text is quite long, and your child may need help and encouragement. It may help if you read the story together and then discuss its content.

Now read part two of the **story** that began on page 12, then answer the questions. ⭐

The Mango Tree (Part Two)

When all the ceremonies were over, and the sister was about to leave with her groom to lead a new life in a new town, she turned to her sister-in-law and said, "Dearest sister-in-law, I'm going to miss my mango tree so much. Would you please do me a great favour and look after it for me? Please water it well and clear the weeds that grow in its shadow."

"Oh, well, yes, yes," answered the sister-in-law.

Once the sister had left, the sister-in-law turned to her husband and yelled, "Did you hear that? Did you hear that? Did you hear your selfish sister? She didn't say that she was going to miss you. She didn't say that she was going to miss me. She *did* say that she was going to miss her mango tree!" She decided then that she was going to ignore the mango tree. The mango tree irritated her just as much as her husband's sister had. Now she could be rid of both.

As the days passed, the unwatered, uncared for mango tree started drying up and its leaves began to fall.

At the same time, the brother, who had been a strong, robust and healthy young man, began to lose his appetite and get thinner and weaker.

One day, a letter arrived. It was from the sister and said, "Dearest brother and sister-in-law. I hope all is well and that my tree is green, and that my brother is in good health."

The remaining leaves of the mango tree were quite yellow by this time, but the sister-in-law wrote back, "Dearest sister. Your tree is fine, but your brother has not been feeling so good."

Soon another letter arrived from the sister. "Are you sure my tree is green? And how is my brother?"

Why did the young man's wife object when his sister said that she would miss her mango tree?
The man's wife felt that his sister cared more about the tree
than she cared about them.

Explain why the young man's wife neglected the tree.
She neglected the tree because she was annoyed with her
sister-in-law and the fuss she had made of the tree.

Which words in the story so far would you use in your own writing, and why?
Answers may vary.

Check your child's understanding of the story by discussing it. Talk about the portrayal of the young man's wife – are her feelings and actions understandable? Ask your child what he or she thinks is likely to happen next.

⭐ ## A traditional story (continued)

Read part three of the **story**, then answer the questions.

The Mango Tree (Part Three)

The mango tree only had one brown leaf on it now, and the brother was so sick that the doctors had said he could not live. So the sister-in-law wrote back, "Your tree is fine, but the doctors have given up all hopes for your brother."

When the sister received this letter, she raced back to her small home town and went straight into the small garden to water her small tree. As she watered it, cleared the weeds around it, and mulched it, it began slowly to turn green.

The brother too, began to recover.

As more leaves returned to the tree, the brother's cheeks got pinker and his eyes became brighter. Within a month, the tree was healthy and strong.

And so was the brother.

It was only then that the sister turned to her sister-in-law and said, "Now do you understand? It was not the tree that I loved, but my brother. It was not the tree whose welfare I was concerned with, but my brother's. The tree and my brother share a common soul. It was my duty to look after them both."

From Seasons of Splendour by Madhur Jaffrey

Can you explain what "the tree and my brother share a common soul" might mean?
It might mean that the tree and the brother were somehow
connected.

How do you think the sister knew that the wife was lying when she said the tree was fine?
The sister knew that the wife was lying because the tree couldn't
be fine if her brother was dying.

Of the three characters in this **story**, whose opinions and feelings do we learn most about?
We learn most about the opinions and feelings of the wife.

Discuss the connection between the brother and the mango tree. What does your child think of this part of the story? It may help if you discuss the questions before your child writes his or her answers.

Your own retelling ⭐

Reread the **story** on pages 12, 13 and 14, then write a **story**, a **letter**, a **monologue** for a play, or a **poem**. Write this from either the **brother's** or **sister's point of view**. You might find it easier if you imagine that you are the **character** you have chosen.

Answers may vary

Your child's story should be narrated by the brother or sister or told from his or her point of view. The National Curriculum for English requires your child to understand that stories can be told from different points of view and that these may influence the reader.

⭐ ## Possessives and plurals

A **possessive apostrophe** shows us who or what belongs to somebody or something.

We usually write **the brothers of Madhur** as **Madhur's brothers**, and we write **the sister of the brothers** as **the brothers' sister**.

The **apostrophe** is always placed after the word that is "owning".
Always add an **-s** if the owner is **singular**.
Always add an **-s** if the owners are **plural** and don't end in an s.
Do **not** add an **-s** if the owners are **plural** and already **end** in an s.

Write the **friend of Thomas** as **Thomas's friend**.
Write the **ball of the boys** as **boys' ball**.

Rewrite the **phrases** below so that they include a **possessive apostrophe**. The first one has been done for you.

the mango tree of his sister	_his sister's mango tree_
the wives of the men	_the men's wives_
the beliefs of the tribe	_the tribe's beliefs_
the fruit of the trees	_the trees' fruit_
the wisdom of the Ancestor	_the Ancestor's wisdom_
the roots of the mango tree	_the mango tree's roots_
the saris of the women	_the women's saris_
the opinion of my sister	_my sister's opinion_
the branches of the trees	_the trees' branches_

These **phrases** work in the same way, although you might not think so! Rewrite them.

in the time of three days	_in three days' time_
in the time of one hour	_in one hour's time_
in the time of two weeks	_in two weeks' time_

The possessive apostrophe can confuse children. However, the National Curriculum for English requires its revision at this stage. Explain that simple plurals (where no "owning" is involved) do not need apostrophes.

Clauses

A **clause** is part of a sentence. A **clause** must contain a **verb** (a doing or being word). The **main clause** in a sentence makes sense on its own; it can usually be written as a sentence by itself. A **subordinate** clause gives further meaning to the **main clause** but does not make complete sense on its own.

Look at this sentence.

As time went by, the people grew weary of hearing the words of wisdom.

The **main clause** is "the people grew weary of hearing the words of wisdom" – it could be a sentence on its own. The **subordinate clause** is "as time went by" – it is not a complete sentence on its own.

Write down the **main** and **subordinate clauses** in the sentences below.

When she received the letter, the sister raced back to the small house in her old home town.

main clause: ...the sister raced back to the small house in her old home town

subordinate clause: When she received the letter

Hoping to hear the words that would ease their misery, the people returned to the great tree again and again.

main clause: the people returned to the great tree again and again

subordinate clause: Hoping to hear the words that would ease their misery

As the days passed, the unwatered, uncared for mango tree started drying up and its leaves began to fall.

main clause: the unwatered, uncared for mango tree started drying up and its leaves began to fall

subordinate clause: As the days passed

This page features an exercise in identifying main clauses in longer sentences. This can be difficult for less-fluent readers who need encouragement to read words in groups rather than singly. Explain that a clause must contain a verb (otherwise it's a phrase).

Understanding poetry

Read this **poem** aloud.

The Rabbit

We are going to see the rabbit.
We are going to see the rabbit.
Which rabbit, people say?
Which rabbit, ask the children?
Which rabbit?
The only rabbit,
The only rabbit in England,
Sitting behind a barbed-wire fence
Under the floodlights, neon lights,
Sodium lights,
Nibbling grass
On the only patch of grass
In England, in England
(Except the grass by the hoardings
Which doesn't count.)
We are going to see the rabbit
And we must be there on time.

First we shall go by escalator,
Then we shall go by underground,
And then we shall go by motorway
And then by helicopterway,
And the last ten yards we shall have to go
On foot.

And now we are going
All the way to see the rabbit,
We are nearly there,
We are longing to see it,
And so is the crowd
Which is here in thousands
With mounted policemen
And big loudspeakers
And bands and banners,
And everyone has come a long way.
But soon we shall see it
Sitting and nibbling
The blades of grass
On the only patch of grass
In – but something has gone wrong!
Why is everyone so angry,
Why is everyone jostling
And slanging and complaining?

The rabbit has gone,
Yes, the rabbit has gone.
He has actually burrowed down into the earth
And made himself a warren, under the earth,
Despite all these people.
And what shall we do?
What *can* we do?

It is all a pity, you must be disappointed,
Go home and do something else for today,
Go home again, go home for today.
For you cannot hear the rabbit, under the earth,
Remarking rather sadly to himself, by himself,
As he rests in his warren, under the earth:
'It won't be long, they are bound to come,
They are bound to come and find me, even here.'

Alan Brownjohn

Listen to your child read the poem. Help your child if he or she finds any parts difficult. This poem is a good example of free verse (unrhymed or irregular verse) that nevertheless has a pattern. Talk about what gives the poem pattern, e.g., the repetition.

Reading and understanding

Reread the **poem** on page 18, then answer the following questions in full sentences.

Is this **poem** about the past, the present or the future? What evidence is there in the poem for your answer?

I can tell this poem is about the future because there is only one patch of grass left in England and only one rabbit.

Why do you think that this is the only rabbit on the only patch of grass?

I think there is no room left for grass and so the rabbits have died out because they had nothing to eat.

What is a hoarding? [D]
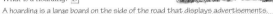
A hoarding is a large board on the side of the road that displays advertisements.

Five ways of travelling are mentioned in the **poem**. What are they? Which is least harmful to the environment?

The five methods of transport in the poem are escalator, underground, motorway, helicopterway and on foot. On foot is the least harmful.

Find the **noun** that names the rabbit's home, then write another word for a rabbit's home. [D]
Remember: A **noun** is a naming word.

In the poem the rabbits home is called a warren. It can also be called a burrow.

Can you name the wild animals that live in a **sett**, an **earth** and a **holt**. [D]

A badger lives in a sett, a fox lives in an earth and an otter lives in a holt.

Why is the rabbit sad?

The rabbit is sad because he is alone and because he can't escape the crowds of people.

In some places rabbits are regarded as pests. What does this mean?

In some places, rabbits eat crops that people have grown.

The questions on this page refer to the poem on page 18. Encourage your child to think about the major issue conveyed by the poem and to form and express opinions on that issue.

Persuasive arguments

Read this example of **informative** and **persuasive** writing.

1 Homes for others
Every living creature has a place where it feels at home. Polar bears are at home in the Arctic; lions at home in the African grasslands. The place where a creature feels at home is called its natural habitat. You feel at home in your own house. You have safe food to eat and you may know your neighbours, even if you are not friends with all of them. It is the same for all other creatures. Their natural habitat is a place where they and their ancestors have lived for perhaps millions of years. They are used to the climate and the other species in the same habitat. Very often wild creatures can only live in one sort of habitat. Conservationists began by saving species which were threatened by stopping hunting, poaching, or overfishing. Now, people realise that saving a species is not enough. Its home has to be saved as well. Natural habitats are in danger everywhere. When people cut down forests or drain swamps the creatures which lived in those habitats may have nowhere else to go.

2 Why conserve?
We are faced with an important decision. We know that thousands of different species are threatened with becoming extinct. Once they are gone, they will never come back. There are probably thousands more in existence that we don't know about because we haven't discovered them yet. Conservation can save some of these species, but costs money and affects people's lives. Why should we bother with it?

3 Looking after ourselves
We need the other creatures in the biosphere because they provide us with food, clothing, building materials, fuel and medicine. However we must use these carefully and sparingly. If we destroy the biosphere because we are greedy or just stupid, then we will die out ourselves. If we look after it, we shall survive, and so will all the other creatures. So conserving the biosphere means looking after ourselves.

From *Endangered Earth* by Jeremy Burgess

What effect do you think the **headings** of the **paragraphs** have on the reader?

The headings clarify what each paragraph is about, emphasising the main points.

Here your child is introduced to informative and persuasive writing. Arguing a case or a point of view and backing it with examples is a useful skill. Help your child realise, however, that such writing is subjective and seldom represents a balanced view.

Writing a summary

Write out as a list the first sentence in each **paragraph** on page 20.

1 Every living creature ....

2 ....

3 ....

Read these sentences again, then **summarise** (write a shortened version of) the writer's argument. Try to write it in 150 words or less, without leaving out any of the main ideas.

Answers may vary

Draw your child's attention to the way the paragraphs in the extract on page 20 each contain a different point. Your child's summary should be a shortened version of the argument that makes sense without reference to the original.

More persuasive writing

Reread the **text** on page 20, then answer the following questions in full sentences.

How does the author explain the term **natural habitat**?

The author explains the term natural habitat as a place where a creature feels
at home.

The author tells you how you feel in your house – but does he really know? Why do you think he does this?

The author doesn't really know how I feel at home. He assumes I feel good because
he wants me to understand how animals feel in their habitat.

The author says that *natural habitats are in danger everywhere*. Is this true or not? Why does he say this?

Not all natural habitats are in danger. The author says that they are to
emphasise his point.

How many times does the author use the words **we**, **us** or **ourselves** in paragraphs 2 and 3? Why do you think he does this?

We = 12, us = 1, ourselves = 2. The author uses these words to make the reader
feel involved.

The author says that if we look after the biosphere, we will survive and so will all the other creatures. Do you think this is definitely true, or can you think of other possible threats to people and animals?

It is not definitely true that if we look after the biosphere we will survive. Other
possible threats include natural disasters and disease.

Write down other **words** or **phrases** (groups of words) that could replace these words in the article without changing its meaning. [D] [T]

poaching illegal hunting ....

extinct dying out ....

biosphere part of Earth where plants and animals live ....

habitat   natural home of a living thing ....

conservation protecting the natural world ....

The questions on this page examine the persuasive text (text that deliberately persuades the reader to the writer's view) on page 20 and reveal how it works. You may need to discuss how to approach the answers if your child is unfamiliar with the topic.

Conservation dictionary

Make your own **conservation dictionary** by collecting words to do with **conservation** and the prevention of **pollution**. Here are some words to start you off.

pollution   conservation   smog   litter   species

waste   atmosphere   fossil fuels   environment

Now find some more words yourself, and write them here. You may want to use **reference books**, the **Internet** or **CD-ROMs** to help you. [T]

....

....

....

Put the **conservation** words in **alphabetical order**, and write a short **meaning** for each one. The **meaning** should be easy to understand. The first one has been done for you. [D]

Word	Meaning
atmosphere	The layer of gases that surrounds the Earth

Answers may vary

Writing definitions of words will ensure that your child comprehends their meanings, which will aid memory and improve his or her vocabulary. Accept any appropriate and easily understood definitions and check that the list is in alphabetical order.

Letter of complaint

Read this **letter**, then answer in full sentences the questions that follow.

Parkview,
Green Lane,
Greenford
11th April

The Chairman,
Greenford Council

Dear Sir,

I am writing to complain about the state of the waste ground, formerly known as Greenford Park, which can be seen from the front of my house.

I use the word "waste" deliberately as this, in truth, is what it has become.

Are we, as local residents, expected to suffer the misuse and probable ruination of this once useful, attractive amenity without expressing our feelings?

For the last month, I have noted the following thoughtless actions that have contributed to its present condition:

- the casual dropping of litter in the form of cans, fast-food packaging, etc.,
- the deliberate dumping of an old mattress,
- damage to the few remaining trees and wild plants from vehicles either crossing the area or parking on it,
- the careless behaviour of dog owners who allow their pets to foul the area without any attempt to clear up the mess that remains, thus endangering public health.

Added to these obvious forms of pollution, there is the noise from portable "music-making" devices in fine weather, which must contribute to the disappearance of the rabbits, badgers and other species from this once beautifully unspoilt wild area.

In these days of conservation and "green" awareness, I should have thought that our council might leap at the chance to create an area that would promote the preservation of plants and wildlife.

Yours faithfully,
Mr I. M. Wild

What is the writer's reason for writing? In which paragraph does he first state his reason?

The writer's reason for writing is to complain about the state of Greenford
Park. He states this in paragraph 1.

Why does Mr Wild use inverted commas around the word "music-making"?

Mr Wild uses inverted commas around "music-making" because he does not
think these machines make real music.

Help your child understand that this letter of complaint is another form of persuasive writing (see page 20). The National Curriculum for English requires the reading and evaluation of this type of letter. You may wish to look at similar letters in a newspaper.

Reading and understanding

Answer the following questions about the **letter** on page 24.

How does the writer suggest that he is writing on behalf of everyone living in Greenford?

The writer suggests he is writing on behalf of everyone living in Greenford by using the words "we" and "the local residents".

How does the writer make clear his four main complaints? What are they?

The writer makes his complaints clear by listing them with bullet points.

He complains about litter, dumping, damage to trees and plants by vehicles and fouling by pets.

Why does Mr Wild use words such as **casual**, **deliberate**, **thoughtless** and **careless**?

Mr Wild uses these words to emphasise the selfishness of the people who damage Greenford Park.

The writer is trying to persuade the council to do something. Which words or phrases suggest this?

The words "in these days of conservation and 'green' awareness I should have thought that our council..." tell us the writer wants the council to help.

Is this just a **letter of complaint**, or does it make any suggestions for improvement? If so, what are they?

The writer suggests that the council makes the Park into an area that will promote the preservation of plants and wildlife, but he does not say how.

A **rhetorical question** is used to make people think, and an answer is not usually expected. Can you find the **rhetorical question** in this **letter** and write it here?

Are we, as local residents, expected to suffer the misuse and probable ruination of this once useful, attractive amenity without expressing our feelings?

Do you think this letter will be successful? Why do you think this?

....

....

....

The questions on this page refer to the letter on page 24. These questions should help your child to understand how language can be used to draw attention to a view and also to manipulate the reader.

Information from posters

Read this **poster**. Decide whether or not it will persuade people to take an interest.

PUBLIC MEETING
In the Village Hall at 7.00 PM
on Wednesday 15th April

OUR PARK IS OUR PROBLEM!

Do you care about:
Our plants and animals?
Natural beauty?
Conservation?

If you really do care then...
Come along to this meeting
Express your views
Sign our petition
Write to your councillor and MP

Something must be done before it's too late!

Now write a short **paragraph** saying what you think is **effective** or **ineffective** about this **poster**.

....

....

....

....

....

....

Your child's paragraph should comment on how well the poster gains attention, informs and persuades. It may help if you first discuss the meaning of the word *effective*. Check your child's writing for clarity and correct grammar and spelling.

Newspaper report

Imagine you are a reporter working for the local paper. You have been asked to write a brief **report** about what happened at the meeting advertised on the poster on page 26. You have limited space for your report, and the editor has already decided on the headline (see below).

You must include:
- when and where the meeting took place
- the name of the chairperson and the number of people attending
- a summary of the views and feelings expressed
- any possible outcomes (what might happen next)

A Public Problem

....

....

....

....

....

....

....

....

....

....

....

....

....

The report should include the four elements listed and be in the style of a newspaper report. Try to look at newspapers and letters with your child. Encourage your child to develop a critical eye rather than to accept everything that he or she reads.

Reading a classic novel

In the nineteenth century, some writers wanted their readers to understand more about the lives of others. In those days before television and the Internet, books were one of the most important ways of **persuading** people to think about the rest of the world.

In Chapters 5 and 17 of his novel *Hard Times*, Charles Dickens describes Coketown, an industrial city in the north of England. Read his description of Coketown in these **extracts**.

It was a town of red brick, or of brick that would have been red if the smoke and ashes had allowed it; ... It was a town of machinery and tall chimneys, out of which interminable serpents of smoke trailed themselves for ever and ever, and never got uncoiled. It had a black canal in it, and a river that ran purple with ill-smelling dye, and vast piles of building full of windows where there was a rattling and a trembling all day long, and where the piston of the steam-engine worked monotonously up and down, like the head of an elephant in a state of melancholy madness. It contained several large streets all very like one another, and many small streets still more like one another, inhabited by people equally like one another, who all went in and out at the same hours, with the same sound upon the same pavements, to do the same work, and to whom every day was the same as yesterday and tomorrow, and every year the counterpart of the last and the next.

... The streets were hot and dusty on the summer day, and the sun was so bright that it even shone through the heavy vapour drooping over Coketown, and could not be looked at steadily. Stokers emerged from low underground doorways into factory yards, and sat on steps, and posts, and palings, wiping their swarthy visages, and contemplating coals. The whole town seemed to be frying in oil. There was a stifling smell of hot oil everywhere. The steam-engines shone with it, the dresses of the Hands were soiled with it, the mills throughout their many storeys oozed and trickled it ... their inhabitants, wasting with heat, toiled languidly in the desert. But no temperature made the melancholy-mad elephants more mad or more sane. Their wearisome heads went up and down at the same rate in hot weather and cold, wet weather and dry, fair weather and foul. The measured motion of their shadows on the walls, was the substitute Coketown had to show for the shadows of rustling woods; while, for the summer hum of insects, it could offer, all the year round, from the dawn of Monday to the night of Saturday, the whirr of shafts and wheels.

You will probably need to help your child read this extract. Reading extracts from classic texts will help familiarise your child with older styles and language and will prepare him or her for reading an entire classic novel in later years.

Reading and understanding ⭐

Answer these questions about the **extracts** on page 28.

Charles Dickens uses more detail than many modern writers would. Why do you think this is?

Unfamiliar scenes had to be described in detail because people did not have TVs

or videos showing pictures of them.

Dickens uses many long sentences and repeats words. What effect does this have on the reader?

It conveys the monotony of Coketown life and gives structure and rhythm to

the text. It is like the rhythm of machinery.

Find as many **adjectives** describing **colours**, **sounds** and **smells** as you can. Write them here.
Remember: An **adjective** is a describing word.

red, black, purple, ill-smelling, rattling, trembling, swarthy, stifling, rustling

....

....

Find a **metaphor** for smoke and write it here.
Remember: A writer uses a **metaphor** to describe something as if it were something else.

Interminable serpents

Find a **simile** for a steam-engine and write it here.
Remember: A **simile** is used to compare one thing with another to create an image in the reader's mind. It often includes the words **like** or **as**.

like the head of an elephant in a state of melancholy madness

Here are some of the words that you may have found unfamiliar or difficult. Draw a line to match each one with its meaning. The first one has been done for you. D

interminable .... very sad
monotonously .... leaked slowly
melancholy .... endless
counterpart .... weakly
wearisome .... same
stokers .... in the same dull way
visage .... furnace feeders
oozed .... boring and tiring
languidly .... face

You may need to discuss some of these questions with your child. You might like to point out that Dickens was a journalist as well as a fiction writer and his novels have an informative and persuasive purpose as well as an entertainment value.

⭐ ## Reading another classic novel

Charles Dickens also wrote _David Copperfield_, a novel about a man's life. As a young boy, David is treated harshly by his stepfather and bullied at school. At the age of ten, he is sent to London to work. Being clever and ambitious, he finds the work very boring. Here, the grown-up David Copperfield describes that particular period in his life.

... I became, at ten years old, a little labouring hind in the service of Murdstone and Grinby.

Murdstone and Grinby's warehouse was at the water side. It was down in Blackfriars ... it was the last house at the bottom of a narrow street, curving down hill to the river, with some stairs at the end, where people took boats. It was a crazy old house with a wharf of its own, abutting on the water when the tide was in, and on the mud when the tide was out, and literally over-run with rats. Its panelled rooms, discoloured with the dirt and smoke of a hundred years, I dare say; its decaying floors and staircase, the squeaking and scuffling of the old grey rats down in the cellars; and the dirt and rottenness of the place; are things, not of many years ago, in my mind, but of the present instant. They are all before me, just as they were in the evil hour when I went among them for the first time. ...

Murdstone and Grinby's trade was among a good many kinds of people, but an important branch of it was the supply of wines and spirits to certain packet ships. ... I think there were some among them that made voyages both to the East and West Indies. I know that a great many empty bottles were one of the consequences of this traffic, and that certain men and boys were employed to examine them against the light, and reject those that were flawed, and to rinse and wash them. When the empty bottles ran short, there were labels to be pasted on full ones, or corks to be fitted to them, or seals to be put upon the corks, or finished bottles to be packed in casks. All this work was my work, and of the boys employed upon it I was one.

Name the **narrator** of this part of the story. D

David Copperfield

Explain the difference between a **narrator** and an **author**. D

The author is the person who writes the book and the

narrator is the character in the book who tells the story.

....

On this page your child reads a second extract by Charles Dickens. Where necessary, help with the reading of the text and the implications of the questions. Encourage your child to compare David's childhood with his or her own.

Reading and understanding ⭐

Answer these questions about the **extract** on page 30.

The third **paragraph** describes the kind of work that the men and boys did. Can you explain briefly what it was?

The men and boys inspected bottles, rinsed and washed them. They also

pasted on labels, fitted corks and seals, and packed the bottles.

Can you complete these **old words** and **phrases** from the extract? They match the meanings of the **modern words** given below. D

Modern word	Old word
next to	ab u t t i n g
rotting	d e c a y i n g
now	of the p r e s e n t i n s t a n t
journeys	vo y a g e s
a lot of	a g r e a t m a n y
results	co n s e q u e n c e s
damaged	f l a w e d
put on	put u p o n

A **hind** was a servant who lived in a house belonging to the master or mistress. Why is this word used in the first sentence?

The word "hind" was used in the first sentence so that the reader knows

David Copperfield's position in the company.

Do you think this **description** gives the reader a good idea of the way David felt? What words can you think of to describe his feelings about his life and work at this time?

The description gives a good idea of David's feelings. He felt the work was

hard, boring and depressing.

You may like to tell your child that Dickens' family went through a period of poverty when he was a child. Use this as a starting point to talk about the influence of a writer's personal experience on his or her writing.

⭐ ## Connectives

Here are some one-word **connectives**.

| and | but | when | because |
| so | for | as | though |

Choose a different one of these **connectives** to link each of the paired sentences below.
Remember: Connectives are words or phrases that link together different parts of a text.
Connectives that link sentences, clauses or parts of phrases are called **conjunctions**.

I fell over. I hurt my knee. _I fell over and I hurt my knee._

The game ended. The referee blew his whistle. _The game ended when the referee_
blew his whistle.

She couldn't ride her bike. It had a puncture. _She couldn't ride her bike because_
it had a puncture.

I couldn't spell that word. I fetched the dictionary. _I couldn't spell that word so_
I fetched the dictionary.

We arrived on time. The train was delayed. _We arrived on time but the train_
was delayed.

Here are some **words** and **phrases** that can also be used as **connectives**.

also however this means for example as this

Fit the **connectives** above into the spaces in these three paragraphs.

Many kinds of words can be used to connect ideas in a piece of writing. _For example_, pronouns, adverbs, and conjunctions are all useful.

This means that we can make our writing more varied and more interesting to read. _Also_, the words we choose can help us to make our meaning clearer to our readers.

However, we should try not to use too many of these connectives in a short piece, _as this_ can make our sentences long and confusing.

Here your child practises using connectives (joining words, phrases or clauses). As your child works through the final exercise, check that he or she understands the meaning of the passage. Don't forget to praise your child's efforts.